Walter Crane

Beauty's awakening: A masque of winter and of spring

Performed in the Guildhall, London, June 1899

Walter Crane

Beauty's awakening: A masque of winter and of spring
Performed in the Guildhall, London, June 1899

ISBN/EAN: 9783337257545

Printed in Europe, USA, Canada, Australia, Japan

Cover: Foto ©ninafisch / pixelio.de

More available books at **www.hansebooks.com**

BEAUTY'S AWAKENING,
A MASQUE OF WINTER AND OF SPRING.

THE STUDIO
SVMMER NVMBER
1899

THE EPISTLE DEDICATORY: TO THE RIGHT HONOURABLE SIR JOHN VOCE MOORE, KNIGHT, LORD MAYOR OF LONDON.

E who have gone so far as to devise and contrive, invent, arrange, and finally bring forth, (with what completeness we may), this our Masque, have even dared further in our boldness, & have added to our so-great risk another as weighty and considerable; which is, that we have ventured to ask (& by your kindness have obtained) leave and permission to set our entertainment before your Lordship, in the presence of the Sheriffs, Aldermen, & leading Citizens of London, and in your own and ancient Guildhall.

WHICH favour, asked by us, and granted by you, goes far in our sight, we would say, to demonstrate two things.

First, that the City (in the persons of your Lordship, & of those who aid you in its governance and careful administration) is as willing to take to-day, as in times past, the position of a chief and foremost supporter and friend to those working in the Crafts and Arts we practice and pursue.

And, secondly, the permission to thus appear before the body of which your Lordship is the head, encourages us, the Art Workers' Guild, to think that that intimate connection between the various Crafts we exercise and the City, that was wont in other times to subsist, is perhaps to be revived and to obtain once more. And this hope we would urge as excuse and cover for presenting before you, this night, our Masque, & of thus re-instituting a custom that prevailed in other and earlier times, though now fallen into unhappy desuetude.

FOLLOWING, though with no too hard and rigid a consistency, the method and manner of the Masque of older and earlier days, not only in the general ordering of our action, but in the particular of the shaping of this Epistle Dedicatory, we would through the means of this latter thank your Lordship for the occasion granted to us for putting forth our Entertainment here and now. Our hope, beforehand, is—with Cicero—(de Orat. I., 3) *Agere cum dignitate et venustate*, and at the close to be able, on your mandate, to say with Plautus—*Operam ludo et deliciæ dedimus*.

WHAT meaning there is in the Allegory that underlies our Action is not far to seek, nor is our Dream an empty, baseless show. We have striven to set forth as well by Poetry and Music as by the various Arts that appeal to and address the eye, that love (on the one hand) of London, our City and (on the other) of the Art we follow, which makes us hope that a day and time will come when, as our City is the greatest in the world, so she shall be the most beautiful, and that, pre-eminent now in commerce, so then shall she also be the leader of cities in the symbolizing of her Greatness by the Beauty of her outward Show.

MOVED and animated, then, by such a hope, we in humbleness and yet in confidence lay before your Lordship our Masque.

                        THE PRESENTERS AND CONTRIVERS.

TO THE CANDID AND GOOD NA-
TURED AUDIENCE.

MASQUE is not a Play and was not a Play, nor could be mistaken for one when the two existed side by side, and we who are submitting the present Pageant & Allegory to your indulgence, wish, at setting out, to insure that you shall not expect things which are not included in our aim.

THERE are certain things more necessary to Masque than they are to Drama, such as Poetic and Ethic Aim, Beauty of Design and Ornament. Ben Jonson was writing masques that cost thousands of pounds (even in those days) to produce, while Shakespeare was acting against a 'back cloth;' or not even so much, as we now use the word.

THE Drama and the Masque did not interchange or overlap; though, later, as we know, a certain Mr. Puff blended a little of the Masque with his tragedy—"a new fancy you know—and very useful in my case." May we express a hope in passing that if our Masque do not set the Thames on fire we may at least succeed in "keeping him between his Banks." The digression may be pardoned: the allusion was too obvious and too tempting for our scribe to resist.

AND though now in our days the Stage has borrowed the Gorgeous Garment of Masque, we feel that there is something still possible to do when Artists who are Designers, but who do not confuse their aim therein with too much attempt at realism and illusion, try to produce an allegory of the Beautiful which is their particular sphere and concern.

DO not, therefore, we would ask you, expect stage illusion or stage perfectness from us—we confess ourselves Amateurs & Pupils in those things; we rather present to you in awkwardly acted shape those Dreams & Fancies which usually form the subject of our Brush and Chisel or other the noble Tools of our Craft.

DESIGN, then, instead of Illusion: something good (we hope) in Form and Colour and Fancy, & something perhaps worth thought in Allegory and Moral Meaning.

AND here let us make a confession: That although the whole scheme is set forth as the wish of us all, yet the several Episodes have been placed in the hands of individuals; & these (artist-wise) have been left very much to themselves in the carrying of their ideas into being.

IN looking at our Patchwork therefore, do not let it jar if scenes differ in character, perhaps with somewhat sudden change; our aim being to produce something wherein, as in a Mediæval Building, the surprising freak of fancy and generally the Unexpected "spoils the proportion and unity of the whole," as he would say who is used to work all things out by square and rule,—" makes the human interest of the whole" we would rather say who hold that Man should be Man. So in judging of our Patchwork (as we have styled it), judge it as you would judge Nature's Mosaics of things Different; for the Sea is not the Land, nor Rocks Trees, yet they go together.

AND even if anything offends you let this thought allay your anger; that it was deemed better to let some strong individualities pass than to hamper an Artist, once his task was assigned to him. There is (we will freely allow it) many a sly hit, or for the matter of that many a bold one, at this or that feature of our many coloured age, which some of us, if we set ourselves to be too sensitive, would feel the Sting of upon our own Backs. And yet the fraternity of our confraternity we are assured will suffer no diminishing by the thrust at these things made by one of the family circle.

AFTER all, that will live which will live; and to put things upon their trial is to put them also upon their mettle; which is good and welcome to all things that have mettle and are worth their trial.

SO we feel it, & so we would ask the indulgent Audience to feel it, when the whip-lash goes round, thinking no more seriously of it than of the Jester's Bladder of Peas and Sword of Lath that wakes the Duller ones in some assembly where dulness is forbid.

AND so we leave ourselves to your Mercy.

BEAUTY'S AWAKENING,
A MASQUE OF WINTER AND OF
SPRING, WRITTEN, DESIGNED &
CONTRIVED BY THE MEMBERS
OF THE ART WORKERS' GUILD,
AND FINALLY PRESENTED BY
THEM IN THE GUILDHALL OF
THE CITY OF LONDON, BEFORE
THE RT. HON. THE LORD MAYOR,
SHERIFFS, ALDERMEN, & COMMON COUNCIL, ON THE TWENTY-NINTH DAY OF JUNE, EIGHTEEN HUNDRED AND NINETY-NINE.

A Citizen (leaping upon the stage): Hold your peace, goodman boy!
Speaker of the Prologue: What do you mean, sir?
Cit.: That you have no good meaning:.... Down with your title boy, down with your title!
S. of Prol.: Are you a member of this noble city?
Cit.: I am.
S. of Prol.: And a freeman?
Cit.: Yea and a grocer.
S. of Prol.: So, grocer, then, by your sweet favour we intend no abuse to the city.
Cit.: No, sir! Yes, sir: if you were not resolved to play the Jacks, what need you study for new subjects purposely to abuse your betters? Why could not you be contented, as well as others, with "The Legend of Whittington" or the "Life and Death of Sir Thomas Gresham, with the building of the Royal Exchange," or the "Story of Queen Eleanor, with the rearing of London Bridge upon woolsacks?"
S. of Prol.: You seem to be an understanding man: what would you have us do, sir?
Cit.: Why present something notably in honour of the commons of the city.

—BEAUMONT AND FLETCHER:
The Knight of the Burning Pestle.

THE CHARACTERS OF THE MASQUE.

TIME: the Speaker of the Prologue.

THE PROLOCUTOR.

THE FOUR WINDS.

THE FOREST LEAVES, DECEMBER, MARCH, & BUTTERFLY.

THE MUSICIANS IN THE DANCE OF THE WINDS.

TRUEHEART: the Seeker.

HOPE.

FORTITUDE.

FAYREMONDE: the Spirit of all things beautiful.

MALEBODEA: a Witch.

ASCHEMON: a Dragon.

THE SEVEN LAMPS OF ARCHITECTURE: in attendance on Fayremonde:
    THE LAMP OF SACRIFICE.
    THE LAMP OF TRUTH.
    THE LAMP OF BEAUTY.
    THE LAMP OF POWER.
    THE LAMP OF LIFE.
    THE LAMP OF MEMORY.
    THE LAMP OF OBEDIENCE.

CLIO: the Muse of History.

THE FAIR CITIES OF THE WORLD: who appear in vision and in pageant before Fayremonde.
    THE FAIR CITY OF THEBES.
    THE FAIR CITY OF ATHENS
    THE FAIR CITY OF ROME.
    THE FAIR CITY OF BYZANTIUM.
    THE FAIR CITY OF FLORENCE.
    THE FAIR CITY OF VENICE.
    THE FAIR CITY OF NUREMBURG.
    THE FAIR CITY OF PARIS.
    THE FAIR CITY OF OXFORD.

IN THE PAGEANT OF THE FAIR CITIES & IN ATTENDANCE UPON THEM.

> RAMESSES II: in attendance upon the fair City of Thebes.
>
> PHEIDIAS: in attendance upon the fair City of Athens, together with two Youths from the Lysis of Plato.
>
> AUGUSTUS: in attendance upon the fair City of Rome, together with three Youths from Mantegna's Triumph of Cæsar.
>
> CONSTANTINE: in attendance upon the fair City of Byzantium, together with St. Helena the Cross-bearer.
>
> DANTE and CIMABUE: in attendance upon the fair City of Florence, together with two Pages as train-bearers.
>
> TITIAN: in attendance upon the fair City of Venice, together with a Doge, two Brides of the Marriage of the Adriatic, and Halberdiers.
>
> ALBERT DÜRER: in attendance upon the fair City of Nuremburg, together with two Train-bearers and a group of Craftsmen from the workshops of Adam Kraft, Hans Sachs, Peter Fischer, and Viansen.
>
> ST. LOUIS & JOAN OF ARC: in attendance upon the fair City of Paris, together with a Herald, and three female figures symbolising the Arts and Graces of Life.
>
> KING ALFRED and WILLIAM OF WYKEHAM: in attendance upon the fair City of Oxford, together with two Acolytes, and a group of Scholars.

LONDON: a City once fair and who at the close of the Masque shall grow fair again.

THE DEMONS ATTENDANT UPON LONDON: of whom seven are deadly Demons but one attains redemption.

> PHILISTINUS: that solid rock of British character whence flow the athletics of sweetness.
>
> BOGUS: who is both ancient and modern.

THE DEMONS (*continued*)

    SCAMPINUS: A most commercial, most plausible, most respectable Demon, whom nobody trusts but everyone believes in.

    CUPIDITAS: whom we all have in our hearts though we fain would disallow it.

    IGNORAMUS: who is first cousin to Philistinus, & though more evil yet in better taste.

    BUMBLEBEADALUS: London's own familiar.

    SLUMDUM: who is worth his weight in gold when he barters for conscience.

    JERRYBUILTUS or JERRY: whom we have cherished so long, and understood so well.

THE VOICE OF THE UNCONSCIONABLE.

THE GENII ATTENDANT UPON LONDON AFTER HER REDEMPTION:

    LABOUR.

    INVENTION.

    FREEDOM.

    COMMERCE.

THE FIVE SENSES: for her enjoyment and wise understanding.

THE SPIRIT OF THE AGE: the Speaker of the Epilogue.

THE DESIGNERS OF GROUPS, SCENES, DANCES, & OTHER PROPERTIES IN THE MASQUE.

THE Masque has been carried out under the general direction of the following Committee of the Art Workers' Guild. The special scenes, dances, & properties being contrived, arranged, designed, or fashioned as stated here below.

Mr. WALTER CRANE, Chairman. Mr. C. R. ASHBEE, Mr. BELCHER, Mr. C. J. HAROLD COOPER, Mr. LOUIS DAVIS, Mr. SELWYN IMAGE, Mr. H. LONGDEN, Mr. MERVYN MACARTNEY, Mr. H. J. L. J. MASSE, Mr. JOSEPH PENNELL, Mr. HOPE-PINKER, Mr. HALSEY RICARDO, Mr. C. HARRISON TOWNSEND, Mr. CHR. WHALL, Mr. H. WILSON.

THE group of the Seven Lamps: Mr. H. Wilson & Mr. Christopher Whall. The Prologue, Time: Mr. C. H. Townsend. The Dance of the Forest Leaves: Mr. Louis Davis. The Pageant of the Fair Cities: Mr. C. R. Ashbee, assisted by Mr. Walter Crane, Mr. Christopher Whall, Mr. E. R. Hughes, Mr. Henry Holliday. The Demons: Mr. Christopher Whall, assisted by Mr. C. R. Ashbee. The Dance of the Senses: Mr. Walter Crane. The Hope and Fortitude Episode: Mr. Walter Crane. The Epilogue: The Spirit of the Age: Mr. Holroyd, assisted by Mr. Walter Crane. The Design for the Prolocutor: Mr. Selwyn Image. The Design and Planning of the Stages: Mr. H. Wilson.

OTHER assistance has been given by members of the Art Workers' Guild as follows: The Design for Clio: Mr. Henry Holiday. The Design of the Throne for London: Mr. W. R. Lethaby. The Design for the Tree: Mr. J. D. Batten. The Designs for Labour & Invention: Mr. G. Moira. The Design for the Dragon: Mr. Walter Crane. The Forest Background: Mr. H. Wilson assisted by Mr. T. M. Rooke. The Director of Musical Arrangements: Mr. J. Belcher. The Assistant Stage Manager: Mr. Harold Cooper. The Chairman of the Publication Committee: Mr. Joseph Pennell. The Sword for Trueheart: Mr. Nelson Dawson. The Sphere and Sceptre for London, and the Clasps for the Robe of Commerce: Mr. Alex. Fisher. The Etching for Time, & other drawings: Mr. Strang. The Dress for Bogus: Mr. A. S. Haynes. The Cutting of the Wood Blocks for the book: Mr. W. H. Hooper. The Designs for the Initial Letters: Mr. C. R. Ashbee. The Lithographs: Mr. T. R. Way. The

Crown and Clasps for London, & the Ship for Commerce: Mr. W. Crane and Mr. C. R. Ashbee. The Capitals for the Proscenium: Mr. Stirling Lee and Mr. Murphy. The Statue in the middle of the Proscenium: Mr. Hope-Pinker. The Couch of Fayremonde: Mr. Wilson. The Lamps: Mr. R. Rathbone. The Leaves in the Forest Scene: Mr. T. R. Spence. The Shield for Trueheart: Mr. A. J. Shirley. The Designs for the Seal for the Art Workers' Guild: Mr. C. J. Harold Cooper. The Printer of the Book: Mr. C. R. Ashbee.

PROFESSIONALS.—Stage Manager: Mr. Hugh Moss. Dancing Master: Signor Espinosa. Composer of the Music: Mr. Malcolm Lawson. The Dance of the Winds: Madame Cavalazzi Mapleson, assisted by Signor Coppi; the music by Mr. Arnold Dolmetsch. Assistant Secretary: Mr. W. H. Ansell.

THE MASQUE.

SCENE   I. THE SLEEP OF FAYREMONDE.

SCENE II. THE QUEST OF TRUEHEART.

SCENE III. THE RALLY OF THE DEMONS.

SCENE IV. THE VISION.

SCENE V. THE AWAKENING.

SCENE VI. THE TRIUMPH.

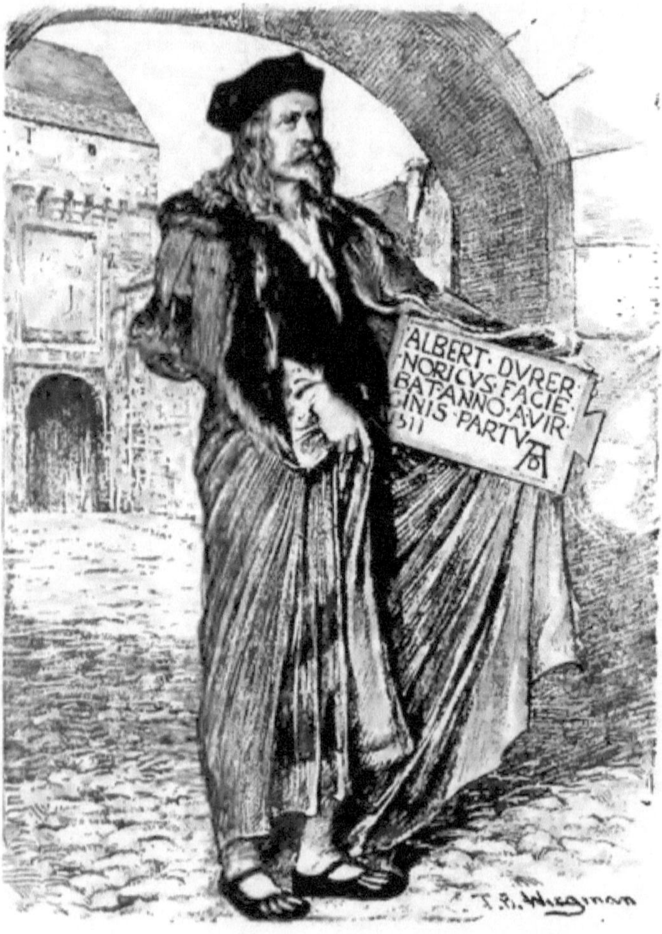
ALBERT · DVRER
NORICVS · FACIE
BAT · ANNO · A · VIR
GINIS · PARTV
1511

THE ACTION OF THE MASQUE.

SETTING FORTH IN ORDER ITS VARIOUS SCENES AND PERSONAGES, TOGETHER WITH SUCH WORDS AS SHALL BE EITHER SPOKEN OR SUNG.

HE Stage being set and arranged after the manner of the ancient Masque-stage has, according to such use and precedent, an inner and an outer scene, space or *pegma*. *(Nihil venustius quam illa pegmata. Cic. Att. 4, 8.)* Of these the backmost or inner, shews, as occasion shall require, a Forest-glade. But, before the opening of the action proper, a curtain being drawn in front of this conceals it, and, for the purpose of the Prologue, the whole of the Stage is in full darkness. Instruments of music play an Introduction, and then, after slight pause, voices without are heard singing the following

RONDEAU.

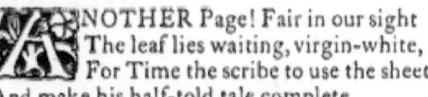NOTHER Page! Fair in our sight
The leaf lies waiting, virgin-white,
For Time the scribe to use the sheet,
And make his half-told tale complete.
Screened from us, secret, hidden quite,
He holds his fateful pen to write
                      Another Page.
Tales blurred with tears will he indite?
Or let the gloom be streaked with light?
Or make a poem, tender-sweet,
Where Life and Hope and Love shall meet?
'Tis Time that knows. He pens aright
                      Another Page!

Towards the end of this song the Stage gradually lightens towards the centre, revealing in half-light Time as Prologue with his emblems of Book, and Scythe, and Glass, who shall speak

A PROLOGUE.

AM the Regent of the Days; my power
Compels in thraldom Æon, Year, and Hour
Into one mighty flux the Ages run,
Past, Present, Future—these and I are one.
The hours, those creatures of the sun and moon,
The timid dawn-time, and the tide of noon,

Slow creeping eve, and sombre stretch of night,
The changing months and seasons in their flight,
The years,—like wavelets of a boundless sea
That form, and break, and straightway cease to be,—
And all the Ages, since the world began,
To me are moments, nay, an instant's span.

AS old as now, I watched the Planets' birth
And shaping of the cosmic fragment—Earth.
I saw the young worlds in their morning prime
While life crept slowly from primordial slime.
As young as now, I still shall hold my sway
When worlds have slowly crumbled to decay;
And when the torches of the night expire
I still shall watch the sinking of their fire!

BUT here, to-night, for one forgetful hour
I doff my kingship, and put off my power.
For a brief space I lay aside my crown,
And, abdicating, cast my sceptre down.
So, by my laws unshackled, you may stand
Within the confines of the Time-less Land,—
The Land of Faery, where all things seem,
Where Man and Time have melted into dream.

Soft music plays as this Prologue is in speaking and after, and at its end the stage slowly darkens, & the figure of Time is obscured by the growing darkness. There is played music, by way of introduction to the Masque proper, and the Spirit of Old Masque, appearing as Prolocutor (*Oratorem voluit esse me, non Prologum*... Ter. Heaut. Prol. II), advances to the front of the stage, and sets forth in verse a forecast of the action and intent of the First Scene as follows:

FAIR Dames and Sirs, in past days may ye know
How guilds of craft presented masque and show,
Seemly in ancient hall, belike as here,
E'en so do we, a Guild of Arts, prepare
A mystery, wherein we would disclose
How Beauty's spirit—soul of life's sweet rose—
In deathly sleep of pale enchantment drear
Doth lie, both she and all her vestals clear.

While Malebodea broods, a shadow o'er her house,
A palace fair hid in a forest close
Of briars and thorns; and from the woodlands-drift
A whirling dance of leaves the wild winds lift,
While in procession move the Seasons four,
With Month by Month across time's silent floor.
If such fair visions may your pleasure meet,
Lend us your willing eyes and patience sweet,
To read what purport deep this masque may hold
Commingling past and present, new and old.

THE FIRST SCENE.
THE SLEEP.

HE inner portion of the Stage shews a tapestried chamber of a Castle or Palace, with an arcade through which is seen the before-mentioned Dark Forest. Fayremonde, the Spirit of All Things Beautiful, is discovered in a profound sleep, upon a couch covered with a rich pall, while a lamp flickers hard by. And round her are grouped her Attendant-maids—the Seven Lamps—each with a lamp which has died out. Their names are Sacrifice, Truth, Power, Beauty, Life, Memory, and Obedience, & they lie in slumber, partly covered with dead leaves which have drifted in from the Forest. Over against the sleeping form of Fayremonde sits Malebodea the Witch, the Weaver of the Spell. Then after music, in which can be heard the piping of the Winds and the murmur of the storm, is sung

THE SONG OF THE WIND AND THE LEAVES.

LOSED around with forest gloom,
  A jewel in a casket hid,
  Sleeps she as on storied tomb,
The golden leaves for coverlid.
Sleep on, sleep on, while these we strew
In fear and hope, till Spring renew.

ARK! In listening forest glade,
  The sea-voiced winds have left their lair
  To weave the shifting shine and shade,
Or lightly lift the Dryad's hair.
Sleep on, sleep still, nor let them bear
Pale thought of trouble to thine ear.

UT we zephyrs with the leaves
  Reckless still of loss or gain
  Play, while Time his dance enweaves
With joy and sorrow, love and pain.
Sleep on, and lightly let them pass
Like cloud-shadows o'er the grass.

INGED dreams we waft her nigh
  Of passèd time and time to come:
  Let painted visions fill her sky
Through the windows of sleep's dome.
Sleep on, nor lightly dream in vain,
Perchance thy dream shall live again.

EAVE the dance with measured paces,
Link our hands to weave the spell
The magic sphere of sleep embraces,
Who may break it? Who shall tell?
Sleep on, sleep on, until the morn
The radiant hunter winds his horn.

Then occurs a dance arranged after the following manner: Young girls representing the Forest Leaves, & sixteen in number, enter in sets of four, and their colours are crimson, brown, orange, and green. The four Winds following them take each his position at a several corner of the stage. Each bears his emblem embroidered on his breast, their habits of various colours. (*For those which Mythologize them chuse some kinde of colour well-suiting with the fable* .... Mont., lib. II., cap. X.) Each wears his insignia, such as the North Wind a golden ship in full sail, the West Wind a cornucopia from which Spring flowers fall, the East Wind thorns & a scourge, and the South Wind a dove & dew-drops powdering his robe. The leaves being impelled and guided by the four Winds from their stations.

The music to this dance is performed upon ancient instruments, the players whereof shall stand upon the stage quaintly attired.

In a pause amid the dancing enters December bearing a star-wand and lantern, and having on either side of her, children representing ice and snow. Then come forth two musicians arrayed as angel and shepherd, & playing carol music while December moves to a stately measure. December having gone out then enters March, armed, and having on either side of him, children representing lambs, whereupon the Four Winds advance and March fights with them. He is overcome, and lies as if dead upon the ground. The two lamb-children then come forward; one takes his sword, and the other, bearing a little red-cross banner, gives it to him, and he straightway comes to life and goes out triumphant. Then takes place a Morris dance, and the Leaves clap their hands, and, as the rows of dancers divide, a little girl runs betwixt them swathed in a brown cloak, which being unwound is butterfly-like within.

In this manner is enacted the title of the Masque, Winter and Spring and Beauty's Awakening.

THE SECOND SCENE.

THE QUEST.

A curtain is painted with trees to represent the forest, and the action takes place on the outer stage. The four Seasons bring in and place in the centre of the stage a tree in blossom. The Prolocutor, from his place, declares the forthcoming action in lines here following:

THE PROLOCUTOR.

WHILE 'neath the witches' spell doth Fayremonde lie,
Trueheart, the Seeker, on his quest doth hie;
Who in the Forest dread, now far astray,
Hath lost in tangled maze his tortuous way.
Weary, he sleeps, while round his slumber weaves
The whirling dance of Winds and Forest leaves.
But in his sleep he hath a vision strange
Of Hope and Fortitude, who bring a change
Like spring, his drooping spirit to requite.
He, lifted by the joy of Beauty's sight—
Seen in his dream—takes courage good
To meet the Dragon fell, in that dark wood
Drawn from his hidden lair—a monstrous birth—
With demons seven making devilish mirth;
Until the Knight's steel smites the snakey scale,
And turns their mockery to dole and wail.

After music the Knight, Trueheart, clad in full armour, enters, bewildered in his quest through the forest, and with his sword broken in hewing a path through the opposing thickets. Wearied and in despair, he presently lies down under the Blossoming Tree, and sleep overtakes him, and in his falling asleep is heard, sung by voices without, the following

SLEEP SONG.

BREATHE soft, ye Winds, and lightly waft
His way-worn soul to calm repose:
Come, poppied Sleep, with kindly craft
Each sense in sealed oblivion close:
Ye fragrant Boughs bend gently down,
Soothing with perfumed charm his rest:
And all ye Spirits of Peace, that own
These woodlands, guard your wandering guest!

SLEEP, gentle Knight, brave heart and true!
    Awhile thy imperious toil forget:
    Or, but in roseate dreams, pursue
The quest whereon thy soul is set.
O radiant Vision, as dew descend
On the parched earth; in beauty steep
His wondering spirit, that nears her end!
Sleep, gentle heart and valiant, sleep.

As he sleeps, music precedes the reappearance of the four Winds and the Forest Leaves, who weave a dance around the Knight. While this is in doing, the Demons—the creatures of Malebodea, the Witch—are discerned lurking in the background, and fitfully appear and reappear.

Then enter Hope and Fortitude from right & left and stand by the sleeping Knight. Hope bends over him as if whispering in his ear words of courage and counsels of endurance, and breaking a spray of the Blossoming Tree places it for encouragement in his helmet. And Fortitude for her part takes from the side of the sleeping Knight his useless weapon—the broken sword—and in its stead places a new one, the Sword of Courage and Conviction Sure. Then the two pointing to the inner scene step aside while the curtain parts, and to the Knight, as in a vision, is disclosed the sleeping Fayremonde with her attendant Lamps. While this is in showing there is sung the following

SONG OF GOOD HOPE.

BE not afraid!
    Seeker, brave and hopeful be.
    Tho' great thy task, and hard for thee,
    Be not dismayed!
Fairness lies hid beneath cold custom's ban
That hides the brotherhood of man with man.
The tangled brakes with Doleful Creatures swarm
While sultry o'er them broods the imminent storm.
And the unhallowed groves with wailing clamour loud
Shudder with blanching leaves against the thunder-cloud.

BUT never did the world long rest
    Content to walk in ways unblest:
    Or nation's thunder rule the waves
Only to guard the Dens of Knaves.
Hearts of goodwill e'en here abide
Whose hopes and prayers are on thy side.

And healing Nature ever fresh and new
That brings each year the spring in seemly show.
With sword in hand and blossom'd crest
And heart renewed renew thy quest;
Drive the dull things of night away
And lead along the young-eyed day!

A great noise is then heard from the depths of the forest. Trueheart, the Knight, awaking, grasps his lately given sword & his shield, and placing on his head the helm on which is displayed the branch of the Tree of Encouragement, prepares to meet this his new foe. Then, with great noise and tumult, enters, as from the wood, a huge & horrid Dragon, Aschemon (*Vidimus immani specie tortuque Draconem* . . . . Cic. de Div. II., 30), and advances to attack the Knight. A great fight ensues. The eight Demons, in alliance with the Dragon, endeavour to thwart and to hinder Trueheart. But he, though greatly spent, at last slays the Dragon, whom being dead, the Demons, lamenting, bear from the stage. Then triumphant music, and Trueheart blows his bugle in token of his victory, and there is sung the following

SONG OF PRAISE.
THE bugle sounds, the monster's slain,
Our lamps shall kindle yet again.
Bring up, oh bring, the gifts of price
To heaven, to heaven the *Sacrifice!*
Let *Truth* reveal, and *Power* hold,
Let *Beauty*, as of yore, unfold
To *Life* that ever throbs to be,
The quickening joys of *Memory*.
Let each reanimated sense
Be chastened to *Obedience*—
Each lamp uplifted let us raise
Our pæan of triumphal praise!

THE THIRD SCENE.
THE RALLY OF THE DEMONS.

The inner scene being again hidden by the curtain, the Prolocutor appears and recites the following lines:

THE PROLOCUTOR.

THE evil brood, though Aschemon is slain,
By Malebodea rallied once again,
Conspire anew against the powers of good.
With mocking dance and song, in hardihood
Rejoicing in their shame, in all despite
Of human spirits striving for the light:
See then the Demons foul, still London's bane.
Intent to blight her realm with blot and stain.
Though yet their hour is brief—the bugle's sound
Strikes palsy to their hearts on Fayremonde's ground.

The Demons are then discovered on the stage, they are cowed and dispondent. To them enters Malebodea, the Witch; as she appears they severally fly hither and thither, but Malebodea beckons them to return. The music tells first of their reluctance, then of their resolution, and when at last they are of one mind they unite in a grotesque and fantastic dance around the Witch. As the dance grows wilder their courage rallies, and their movements grow more expressive of what they still shall dare to do. At the close of all there is a great shout taken up without; this is the climax, as it dies away there is heard a voice—minatory, accusatory, plaintive, mocking, the voice of conscience, the voice of human destinies, the voice of the unconscionable, and thus shall the voice speak, denouncing each Demon as in his turn he is summoned to stand forth, & at the close of each denunciation the chorus takes up the refrain.

THE VOICE: Stand forth Philistinus!

WOE for the world that has loved to define us!
Shall it repine us, must it resign us,
Must every Bayswater dinner be minus
The soapy punctilious old sneak Philistinus?
Old sneak did I say? Kind friends—draw it easy!
Philistinus is buoyant, and beefy and breezy.
By the Huddersfield weavers, the Manchester spinners,
By all the brave bagmen that bung for their dinners,
The Glasgow distillers, the Macclesfield fullers,
By —(well never mind!) with his coat of bright colours!
Philistinus his missions, his gunboats, his traders,
Bears the banner of exploit for modern crusaders—

By everything holy, commercial and cunning,
Philistinus, the British, comes first in the running.

HUFFLE, and soft soap, and slipshod, and sham;
Culture and cram; cant in the jam,
Press-puff and persiflage, humbug and flam,
All to Dance to the Dance of the Devil's own Dam!

THE VOICE: Stand forth Bogus.

WOE to the World, if no longer it pays
Its tribute to Bogus the Ancient of Days—
What! Dare the World venture to check at the phrase?
Or deny ME, its Master, that guides its displays,
And its destiny sways,
If not 'ab initio' at least in these days—
Pray what will become of its crotchets and craze,
Its conventional ways, its starch and its stays,
Its upholstered plays, its R.I.B.A.'s,
Or even its Laureates' Bogus bays
Schoolboards that birch with a Bogus rod,
Chemical peas in a Bogus pod.
Bogus politics, (wasn't it odd
How lamely our liberal leaders were shod,
When the last Bogus plank of their platform was trod!)
Bogus Art, and a Bogus God!
Down with you Bogus under the sod!
Hocus, pocus, bottomless Bogus!
Shall a Puritan Jabez no longer berogue us?—
Pounding along on a guinea pig's back,
His cant and his companies all gone crack;
Bogus shall howl with the rest of the pack!

HUFFLE, and soft soap, and slipshod, and sham;
Culture and cram; cant in the jam,
Press-puff and persiflage, humbug and flam,
All to Dance to the Dance of the Devil's own Dam!

THE VOICE: Stand forth Scampius!

AYE and Scampinus, the Sharp and the Flat,
With his solemn sabbatical black cravat,
His immaculate togs, and his silk top hat,
His fortune in pills, and the affable chat,
Of his puff in the Press, for he pays for that,
As he pays for his complaisant aristocrat,—

His margarine pat, and the drugs in his vat,
And his spicy bread sausages, flavoured with cat.
East and West would you give of the best,
And reap of the worst, Scampinus you pest?—
Plugson of Undershot standing confessed!
With the soul of a ghoul and the teeth of a rat,
Scampinus accursed, come away with the rest.
    HUFFLE, and soft soap, and slipshod, and sham;
    Culture and cram; cant in the jam,
    Press-puff and persiflage, humbug and flam
    All to Dance to the Dance of the Devil's own Dam!

THE VOICE: Stand forth Cupiditas!

AYE, and Cupiditas rank as a weed,
That sprouts in the dung from a sodden seed.
Not fair as of old was the Lady Mead
But sordid with utilitarian greed,
Your devilish dividend-hunting avidity,
Claws all alike with impartial placidity;
For the Shark with his Company-cadging cupidity
Can match Ignoramus' solid stupidity.
You are spawned on the Vestries and Boards where you breed
For an ever devouring Democracy's need,
You'd sell Westminster Abbey and God, to feed!
The poor, as of old, on Iscariot's creed!
Shuffle Cupiditas off with speed
To join in the dance of the Devil's stampede.
    HUFFLE, and soft soap, and slipshod and sham;
    Culture and cram; cant in the jam,
    Press-puff and persiflage, humbug and flam,
    All to Dance to the Dance of the Devil's own Dam!

THE VOICE: Stand forth Ignoramus!

DOES anyone shame us, or saucily name us?
Who by the Gods of Convention dare blame us?
Sure as M.P. and Councillor well he became us
Our dear, platitudinous, far-hearing, famous,
Firm, British-matronly Ignoramus?
Ignoramus, the pity, the pity!
Shall you maunder no more your infallible ditty,
As you loaf in the slum, or lounge in the City,
Or lead the Academy hanging Committee,
Or inflate John Bull with your self-reliance,

Or hug your departments of Art and Science?
Shall your pride and your prurience no more inflame us?
Down with you, Down with you, Ignoramus!

HUFFLE, and soft soap, and slipshod and sham;
Culture and cram; cant in the jam,
Press-puff and persiflage, humbug and flam,
All to Dance to the Dance of the Devil's own Dam!

THE VOICE: Stand forth Bumblebeadalus!

OOM for this picturesque waxwork of Dædalus,
Room for the London of old Bumblebeadalus!
The London of vestries, of jobs and of lies,
Of puffs and of posters, of signs in the skies,
Of crawling busses and crowded trains,
Of river monopolies, unflushed drains,
Would you be-wheedle us old Bumblebeadalus?
Our London, the joyless, the reckless of brains,
The sleepy, the smoky, the sooty remains!
And what if a tub-thumping socialist boggles
At your mace and your furs and your gloves and your goggles,
Old Bumble grows bigger, his heart merely hardens
As he crawls from the Mansion House into Spring Gardens,
For now he's but added, the more to prevail,
To his blustering tongue, a sting to his tail;
With his twists, and his shifts, and his betterment schemes,
His technical education dreams,
His cooked accounts, and his legal quirks,
His legacies from the Board of Works,
The reforms he gases about but shirks.
No Bumblebeadalus, you'll not be-wheedle us!
Though you give Mrs. Grundy a wreath of myrtle,
Sing premature threnodies over the Turtle,
Not all the 'i's' Mac*****l dots,
Not all the pennies in all the slots,
Not all J**n B***s' random shots,
Not W***'s municipal melting pots,
Not B*****d S***'s most cynical plots
Shall make old Bumble change his spots!
But a City whose name shall descend into story
As we picture her greatness or sing of her glory,
Who shall stand as a joy to the proudest of nations,
Such a city comes not in your calculations,
And the treasures and charms that might make her agen

What she once was to Eveleigh or Christopher Wren,
Old Bumble regards but as empty frivolities,
Old Bumble has universal qualities;
Off, off, you old reprobate—you'll not pronounce ill
On the change from King Log to King County Council!

> HUFFLE, and soft soap, and slipshod and sham;
> Culture and cram; cant in the jam,
> Press-puff and persiflage, humbug and flam,
> All to Dance to the Dance of the Devil's own Dam!

THE VOICE: Stand forth Slumdum!

> LUMDUM come, you must come with the rest of them,
> Whitechapel horrors the goriest and best of them,
> Blistering profanity fleshing a zest of them,
> Cent-per-cent. rentals and lawyers in quest of them,

Shelters and pawnshops and preachers—a pest of them—
Street organ, gin palace, all gone mum!
Stop thumping your damned philanthropical drum,
And into the limbo come, Slumdum come!

> HUFFLE, and soft soap, and slipshod and sham;
> Culture and cram; cant in the jam,
> Press-puff and persiflage, humbug and flam,
> All to Dance to the Dance of the Devil's own Dam!

THE VOICE: Stand forth Jerry!

> AND shall the ubiquitous Jerry come too?
> Come with his girders and "bays for a view?"
> Jerry the fanciful, Jerry the true,
> Jerry the merry, the artful, the new,

Jerry the semi-detached, two by two,
Little Pedlington Mayors, and District Surveyors,
Microbe tanks, drain-pipes, and Typhoid purveyors,
Cadging along with the rest of the crew,
Off into Jericho Jerry goes too!

> HUFFLE, and soft soap, and slipshod and sham;
> Culture and cram; cant in the jam,
> Press-puff and persiflage, humbug and flam,
> All to Dance to the Dance of the Devil's own Dam!

The dance and the music have grown wilder and madder; at the close of all there is heard again on a sudden the clarion of Trueheart, whereupon all disperse and the scene closes.

THE FOURTH SCENE.
THE VISION OF FAYREMONDE.

The Prolocutor from his place sets forth the forthcoming action in the lines here following:

THE PROLOCUTOR.

    WHILES doth the Knight the darksome forest range
    Upon the Sleep of Fayremond draws a change,
    When turns the storied sphere of dreams controlled
    By Clio, stately dame who hath enscrolled
The world's fair lore. And she doth summon there
The images of cities nine most fair,
As they in primal beauty decked the earth,
When shone the slumbering lamps, and joy had birth
In all man's labour, as with craft and art,
Each thing of use had life to cheer the heart,
And pictured walls emblazoned mighty deeds
With all the people's lore, for daily needs.
Cinctured in mutual service, walled and towered
Behold their semblance—each a bride rich dowered.

Fayremonde, cast by spell and enchantment into a deep sleep, is supposed therein to see, as in a vision, a display, in manner of procession, of those Fair Cities, which in olden days belonged to her realm, and owned her sway and governance. The scene being the inner, and arranged after the manner of the First Scene, these enter, each accompanied by a worthy & noble citizen, ruler or artist, famous & notable in the palmy days of such city. To set these forth in their order they are: Thebes, attended by Ramesses II.; Athens, by Pheidias and two youths from the Lysis of Plato; Rome, by Augustus & three youths from Mantegnas Triumph of Cæsar; Byzantium, by Constantine and St. Helena the Cross-bearer; Florence, by Dante & Cimabue, with two Pages as train-bearers; Venice, by Titian, with a Doge, two Brides of the Marriage of the Adriatic & Halberdiers; Nüremburg, by Dürer, two Train-bearers & a group of Craftsmen from the workshops of Adam Kraft, Hans Sachs, Peter Fischer, & Viansen; Paris, by Saint Louis & Joan of Arc, a Herald and three female figures symbolising the arts & graces of life; Oxford, by King Alfred & William of Wykeham, two Acolytes & a group of Scholars. As these severally enter there is recited such one of the following stanzas as appertain to each city:

THEBES.

    YOUNG was the world that saw me, Thebes, arise,
    Serene in wisdom, and in state serene:
    Sphinx-like I sat, and watched with fateful eyes

Myriad on myriad slaves salute me Queen.
Deep to earth's core I tracked her secret ways,
And charmed the majestic heavens to crown my praise.

ATHENS.
 WISDOM was mine, and Beauty: mine the Joy
 Sprung from their fathomless depths withdrawn, serene:
 Nor while the world endures shall age destroy
The seal and dominion of my gracious mien.
Lo! violet-crowned, a Queen 'neath cloudless skies,
Full on Perfection gazed my faultless eyes.

ROME.
 I WAS the Mistress of the World; on me
 The gods had laid the imperial soul for dower.
 I came, I saw, I conquered earth and sea,
And from my touch sprang desert lands to flower.
Chaos before me fled, and girt with awe
Deep in men's hearts I set the throne of Law.

BYZANTIUM.
 I WAS the daughter of imperial Rome,
 Crowned by her Empress of the mystic East:
 The Most Holy Wisdom chose me for her home,
Sealed me Truth's regent, and high Beauty's priest.
Lo! when Fate struck with hideous flame and sword,
Far o'er the new world's life my grace outpoured.

FLORENCE.
 FLORENCE am I, the peerless Flower of all,
 The blood-red Lily borne on Arno's wave!
 I am the Bride of Art, the imperial
Mistress of Beauty, for whom Dante gave
His heart's blood; and grave Buonarotti's spell
Enchained the world within my citadel.

VENICE.
 BORN of the Sea was I, yea, born of the Sea,
 When the young Dawn first kissed and turned to rose
 Her orient pearl. Majestic, strenuous, free,
Calm in my soul, I feared no mortal foes.
Back to their East the Crescent hordes I hurled:
And Europe breathed once more, a rescued world.

NUREMBURG.

STRONG as the sun, fair as the rose in June,
For Duty and Beauty all my soul afire;
Life's chords discordant trained to perfect tune,
Deft hands, stout heart, knit fast to one desire:
Sound to the core, self-centred, buoyant, free,
I bore my sons to Toil and Liberty.

PARIS.

LO! 'neath these northern skies enthroned, on me
Art set her daintiest touch, and charmed my hand
To deftest cunning and felicity,
Since her last radiance sank o'er Grecian land;
Gay as an April morn Love's kisses thrill
I hold men's hearts in thraldom at my will.

OXFORD.

RUDE was this land, when lo! my spirit rose
At Alfred's summoning by Isis' shore;
And the Eternal Wisdom bade unclose
In Oxford's halls her grave, mysterious lore.
Ah! yet, poor World, thy weary soul desires
The secret spells that haunt my dreaming spires!

Moving to a stately march, they all, in turn, bow to Fayremonde, & pass away, leaving her still wrapt in her magic slumber, & as they are leaving, the Prolocutor, from his place, speaks the following words:

THE PROLOCUTOR.

ONE yet remains, in mean attire, distrest,
Though holding riches more than all the rest—
E'en London, blackened with the smoke of toil
And luxury, and tangled in the moil
Of penury and care, mid wealth untold,
With rich historic garment torn and old—
Creature of shreds and patches, yet a queen,
By Demons fell tormented and made mean.
For her deliverance may we hope and pray
That she, a city fair, may rise one day.

Towards the close of these verses enters hurriedly, London, pursued by the eight Demons who torment her. After which they leave the stage, & the curtain falls over the inner scene.

THE FIFTH SCENE.
THE AWAKENING.
The Prolocutor from his place sets forth the forthcoming action in the lines here following:

THE PROLOCUTOR.
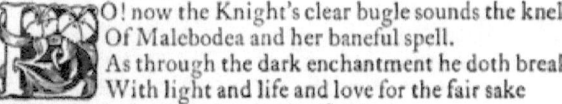O! now the Knight's clear bugle sounds the knell
Of Malebodea and her baneful spell.
As through the dark enchantment he doth break
With light and life and love for the fair sake
Of Fayremonde, with the magic of a kiss
Won to the world that her did sorely miss:
Rekindle each fair vestal's sacred flame
Whose light the powers of darkness hence shall shame,
And bring joy back upon the sun's warm beams
To re-create the garden of youth's dreams,
Wherein the Senses Five their dance renew,
As shall appear forthwith in order due.

The inner scene is set out as in the first scene. The sound of the Knight's bugle horn is heard from the depths of the forest. Malebodea starts and rising to her feet looks around in affright as if for help. To her then enter the Demons; they gather round their protectress, capering grotesquely. Trueheart, the Knight, enters, his sword being drawn, and with the air of a victor, and confronts the Demons & Malebodea, and breaking through them while they cower back on either side of the stage, he enters through the arcade, and approaching the couch of Fayremonde, bends over her in wonderment & in happy satisfaction at the conclusion of his quest. There is then sung, by voices without, the

SONG OF THE AWAKENING.
AKE, lovely maid, thy foes no more withhold me!
Loosed is the spell that long enchained thine eyes,
Now may the healing from thy glance enfold me,
Wake, sweet one, wake, and make me wise!

IM shews the golden earth while thou art sleeping,
Faint in our hearts thy Beauty's image lies,
Weary the watch the waiting lamps are keeping,
Wake, sweet one, wake, our hope else dies.

O more Aschemon's coil may bar or bound thee,
No more Mal'bodea's might compel thy sighs,
Fayremonde thy Trueheart's arms at last are round thee,
Wake, sweet one, wake, I kiss thine eyes!

And Trueheart the Knight taking from his helm the spray of blossom, bends over the sleeping Fayremonde & wakes her with a kiss. The spell being broken she rises in happy wonder from her long trance. The Seven Lamps the while awake and re-kindle their extinguished flames.

Then enter, as a sub masque, to symbolize the awakening of beauty and the joy of life renewed, five couples richly attired, the colours of their raiment displaying the colours of the rainbow in order. Each pair represent respectively the Senses of Hearing, Seeing, Tasting, Smelling, and Touching, and bear proper emblems. Each sense is illustrated in turn in the movements of the dance which follows and closes the scene.

THE SIXTH SCENE.
THE TRIUMPH.

The Prolocutor from his place speaks as follows:

PROLOCUTOR.

NOW in achievement new the spirits rare
Of Labour and Invention draw and bear
The seat of amity and power. Here throned
Shall Fayremonde sit with Trueheart, while atoned
Shall London's penance be, the Demons stayed,
And she recovered—most fair arrayed,—
With Freedom and rich Commerce take her place
With her fair sisters of the past, and grace
The Court of Truth and Beauty, evermore
As one—through changing forms of Art the core
Of Life; beneath whose sway fresh from the dews
Of Strife and Hope the weary world renews
Her youth. Then shall the Spirit of the Age
Recite the Epilogue and close the page.

The characters are discovered in place as at the end of the last scene. A Triumphant March is played, while a fair seat is then brought in by Labour and Invention and placed under the arch of the inner scene. Then Fayremonde led by Trueheart, is enthroned on it, he standing at her right hand. In attendance upon Fayremonde are the Seven Lamps & the Five Senses. All these having taken their places, then shall enter London torn and dishevelled, still pursued by the Demons. She kneeling at the feet of Fayremonde sues for help. Trueheart at her appeal draws his sword and confronts the Demons, who, hesitating in their attack, are preparing to slink off, but the Lamps close in on them crescent-wise, and Simplicity & Goodwill drive forward Cupiditas, Scampinus, Ignoramus, Bogus, and Jerrybuiltus with scourges up to the glass of Truth, before which they cower and shrink. Of the three other Demons meanwhile, Philistinus stands stolidly looking on; Bumblebeadalus and Slumdum pulling their official and hypocritical robes respectively about them, stand, taking sides with the powers of good, and sneakingly applauding the confusion and condemnation of the others. These latter are driven off the stage in disgrace as aliens, and the other three who are moving off also, are arrested and brought up for judgment. The robes of Bumblebeadalus and Slumdum are stripped off by the Cherubs who then scourge the naked and wingless creatures round and off the stage. Finally with a burst of impotent rage Malebodea the Witch likewise rushes off.

Then enter the Fair Cities with their attendants, and doing homage to Fayremonde and Trueheart, they also take their places and form a court. London, who, during the passage with the Demons, had withdrawn herself under the protection of Fayremonde's court, now re-enters, her aspect changed, and being clad in a fair, rich emblazoned mantle, she is led by Freedom and Commerce and enthroned opposite to Fayremonde (whose seat has meanwhile been moved to the side of the stage). She then receives from Labour and Invention a crystal sphere and a sceptre, and so takes her place as a Fair City among the Fair Cities. Then may be sung the following:

SONG OF TRIUMPH.

ALL is done!
All is won!
Doubt and fear no more confound us:
Rising hopes renewed surround us:
Rising day
Drives night away,
Morning throws its beams around us,
Making summer holiday.
Heaven sends Nature down to us again,
Renewing our dull Earth like summer rain.

IS there hope?
Is there hope?
What see the hills that gird our city round,
And take large outlook of our English ground?
Far to the verge where rolls our sea
That clasps us in its arms and keeps us free;
But on the hither side,
Narrowing the prospect wide,
Look into one dim pit of smoke and flame
Where boils and fumes our strength and pride and shame,
Where hearts of gold are melted into dross,
And hearts of earth are beaten into gold,
And, streaming like a tide, the gain and loss
Beat to and fro
With ceaseless ebb and flow,
Writing the tragedy of young and old.
Where bright-eyed lives are caught and stricken blind,
And stifled in the nets of greed,
And bought and sold;

Or, if perchance their feet are freed,
Rush on in abject fear of being left behind.

WAKE again!
O wake again!
Heart of our English land that lies asleep,
And show us, on the other side the steep,
All round, the fair Champain.
For Rome might die yet Italy remain,
And shall we say, who hear our cities weep,
Our sands are also run?
Our day nigh done,
That cold decay
Draws its twilight veil of gray
Before our sun?
O rather say,
That year by year, within the purple main,
Our land renews its strength again
As spreads the spring once more
With coy delayings along the northern shore;
And, day by day,
Morning rises grave or gay
And sometimes brings as with the dawn,
The Baltic cold with daggers drawn
That sweeps the landscape gray,
And sometimes a fairer scene
Where falls the sun on meadows green
While the south-west leads out the lambs to play.

ALL these things remembering,
We, the children of the changing clime,
That trains our spirits to be great,
And take the unreckoned chances of our fate,
And meet the varying time,
Together sing
Our tale of winter and of spring,
And play our mime of Beauty's wakening.

WAKEN then
Spirit of Beauty! once again.
Lead with new hope our aimless feet along!
"Teach us our trade!" the children cry;

"Show us our way and force us to be strong!
"And though the sunshine never tarries long
"To slack our wills,
"Yet point a clearer path on fresher hills,
"Beneath a kinder sky!"

Then shall the Spirit of the Age appear as a cloaked figure with winged cap and wings upon his feet, having a scroll and pen in one hand & holding aloft a search-light in the other. He advances to the centre of the stage and at its very front shall then recite the following verses as

EPILOGUE.

IME claim thine own! Our little hour is o'er;
Thy things that are, replace our things that seem,
And re-assert thy kingly power once more
And take as thine our Vision and our Dream.

HOUGH thine the withered petals of the rose,
Thine the dead glories of its scent, its hue,
Yet ours the buds that burgeon and disclose
Fresh hopes that still shall live, and still renew.

UR hopes are left; for Hope and Art are one:
Young Hope, young Art, each holding hand of each,
Our pictured fancy fled, Time's world begun,
Hope is the lesson that our dream shall teach.

Which said he leads all the company forth in procession. And they shall march round the stage, triumphant music playing the while, & descend into the hall, passing down an aisle through the audience to the further end of the hall and returning to the stage, where

EXEUNT OMNES.

THE AUTHORS, AIDERS AND ABETTORS OF THE ABOVE LITERATURE WHO HAVE CONSPIRED TOGETHER TO ASSAULT THE PUBLIC CONFIDENCE WITH THEIR PATCHWORK; BLUSHING TO APPEND THEIR NAMES, EACH AT THE FOOT OF HIS PIECE; YET MANFUL TO UNDERTAKE THE RESPONSIBILITY FOR THEIR WORK (LEST IT SHOULD, HAPLY, BE WRONGLY ASCRIBED & THUS SHOULD WEIGH ON THE WRONG SHOULDER) HAVE SUBSCRIBED THEMSELVES WITH CERTAIN MARKS, WHICH THEY HERE CLAIM AS THEIR OWN, AND IN THUS SAYING FAREWELL, WOULD, IN THE MANNER OF THE OLD SCRIBES, BEG EACH HIS SHARE IN THE CHARITABLE CONSIDERATION OF THE READER.

 C. R. ASHBEE.

 WALTER CRANE.

 SELWYN IMAGE.

 C. HARRISON TOWNSEND.

 C. W. WHALL.

 H. WILSON.

THE FOREGOING LETTERPRESS SET UP FOR THE ART WORKERS' GUILD AT THE PRESS OF THE GUILD OF HANDICRAFT, LIMITED, ESSEX HOUSE, BOW, UNDER THE SUPERVISION OF C. R. ASHBEE, JUNE, EIGHTEEN HUNDRED AND NINETY-NINE.

THE CHARACTERS OF THE MASQUE.

TIME	Mr. C. Harrison Townsend.
THE PROLOCUTOR	Mr. Selwyn Image.

THE WINDS
N. Wind	Mrs. Ledward.
W. Wind	Miss E. Cooke.
E. Wind	Miss L. Chaplin.
S. Wind	Miss Parkhouse.

MARCH	Master Harold Beaumont.
DECEMBER	Miss Enid Ledward.

MUSICIANS IN DANCE OF WINDS.
TRUEHEART	Mr. Paul Woodroffe.
HOPE	Miss Brend.
FORTITUDE	Miss Standage.
FAYREMONDE	Miss Alexander.
MALEBODEA	Miss Brandon.
ASCHEMON, the Dragon	Mr. Lancelot Crane.

THE SEVEN LAMPS.
Memory	Miss Chaplin.
Beauty	Mrs. Clarke.
Truth	Miss Walker.
Power	Miss Woodcock.
Sacrifice	Miss Grace Knewstub.
Obedience	Miss Boone.
Life	Mrs. Grant.

CLIO: The Muse of History	Miss Helena Head.

THE FAIR CITIES.
Thebes	Mrs. Wheeler.
Athens	Miss Wackermann.
Rome	Mrs. Bishop.
Byzantium	Miss D. Wolner.

THE FAIR CITIES (continued):
    Florence   Miss Ashbee.
    Venice   Mrs. C. R. Ashbee.
    Nuremburg   Miss Johnstone.
    Paris   Mrs. Oakley Williams.
    Oxford   Miss Harwood.

WORTHIES IN ATTENDANCE ON THE CITIES.
    Thebes: Rameses   Dr. Wheeler.
    Athens: Pheidias   Mr. F. W. Pomeroy.
        Grecian Youths   Mr. C. Downer.
                                   Mr. A. S. Tuckey.

    Rome: Augustus   Mr. F. Madox Hueffer.
        Roman Youths   Mr. J. Bailey.
                                   Mr. A. Pilkington.
                                   Mr. Lewis Hughes.

    Byzantium: Constantine   Mr. Gerald Moira.
        St. Helena   Miss May Morris (Mrs. Sparling).

    Florence: Dante   Mr. Douglas Cockerell.
        Cimabue   Mr. Arthur Cameron.
        Trainbearers   Master Tom Ireson.
                                   Master Gilbert Ledward.

    Venice: The Doge   Mr. M. White.
        Titian   Mr. Hugh Stannus.
        Two Brides of the   Miss Trust.
            Adriatic   Mrs. Douglas Cockerell.
        Three Halberdiers   Mr. G. F. Loosely.
                                     Mr. C. H. B. Quennell.
                                   Mr. J. Pyment.

    Nuremburg: Albert Dürer Mr. Walter Crane.
        Trainbearers   Master Olaf Caröe.
                                   Master Whall.
        Craftsmen   Mr. Cyril Kelsey, Goldsmith.
                                   Mr. H. Ponting, Brazier.
                                   Mr. C. H. Holden, Brazier.
                                   Mr. Austin Gomme, Mason.
                                   Mr. Sidney Cotton, Blacksmith.
                                   Mr. A. G. Rose, Cobbler.

WORTHIES IN ATTENDANCE ON THE CITIES (continued):

Paris: St. Louis	Mr. E. R. Hughes.
Joan of Arc	Miss Susan Cox.
Herald	Miss Caröe.
Three Arts and Graces	Miss Metchim.
	Miss Netter.
	Miss Stone.
Oxford: King Alfred	Mr. C. J. Harold Cooper.
William of Wykeham	Mr. C. W. Whall.
Acolytes, Scholars, &c.	Master Whall.
	Master H. Edwards.
	Master Fred Brooks.
	Master Fred Rhead.
	Mr. H. R. Thomas.
	Mr. J. W. Barnes.
London	The Baroness de Bertouche.

DEMONS.

Philistinus	Mr. H. Longden.
Bogus	Mr. A. S. Haynes.
Scampinus	Mr. H. M. Fletcher.
Cupiditas	Mr. C. C. Brewer.
Ignoramus	Mr. T. R. Spence.
Bumblebeadalus	Mr. O. N. Ayrton.
Slumdum	Mr. A. H. Macmurdo.
Jerrybuiltus	Mr. C. Spooner.

THE FIVE SENSES.

Sight	Miss G. Parnell.
	Mr. G. F. Metcalfe.
Hearing	Mrs. Caröe.
	Mr. W. D. Caröe.
Smell	Miss G. Reynolds.
	Mr. Lionel Crane.
Taste	Miss Fawsett.
	Mr. N. Evill.
Touch	Miss Oswald.
	Mr. F. Inigo Thomas.

THE VOICE OF THE UNCONSCIONABLE.

LABOUR	Mr. P. Fielding.
INVENTION	Miss Maud Ritchie.
FREEDOM	Miss B. Crane.
COMMERCE	Miss Young.

THE SPIRIT OF THE AGE   Mr. Stacy J. Aumonier.

FOREST LEAVES
                Miss Una Cockerell.
                Miss L. Aman.
                Miss Phyllis Beaden.
                Miss Maude Brooks.
                Miss Queenie Cross.
                Miss Janet Hird.
                Miss Phyllis Logan.
                Miss Stella Margetson.
                Miss Beryl Mount.
                Miss Van Duryer.
                Miss E. Van Duryer.
                Miss Stella West.
                Miss Evelyn West.
                Miss Veronica Whall.
                Miss Hilda Ledward.

THE GUILDHALL.

1. EXTERIOR. AUTOLITHOGRAPH BY T. R. WAY.
2. EXTERIOR. BY JOSEPH PENNELL.
3. INTERIOR LOOKING EAST. BY JOSEPH PENNELL.
4. INTERIOR LOOKING WEST. BY JOSEPH PENNELL.
5. ENTRANCE. BY C. J. WATSON.

THE STAGE AND ITS ACCESSORIES.

6. THE STAGE. AUTOLITHOGRAPH BY HENRY WILSON.
7. PLAN OF THE STAGE. BY HENRY WILSON.
8. THRONE OF IVORY. BY W. R. LETHABY.
9. CAPITAL OF ONE OF THE COLUMNS. BY HENRY WILSON.
10. CAPITAL OF ONE OF THE COLUMNS. BY HENRY WILSON.
11. SWORD FOR TRUEHEARTE. BY NELSON DAWSON.
12. THE SCEPTRE FOR "LONDON." BY ALEX. FISHER.
13. CLASP AND KEYS FOR "LONDON." BY C. R. ASHBEE.
14. SHIELD FOR TRUEHEARTE. BY A. J. SHIRLEY.

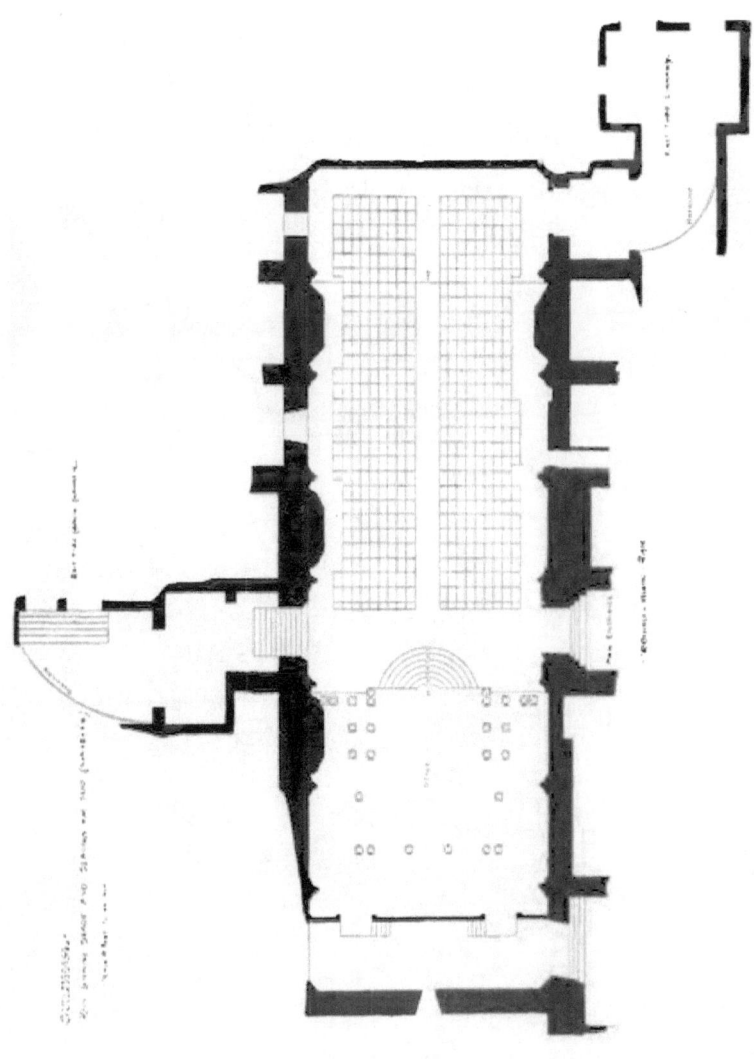

CAPITAL TO ONE OF STAGE
COLUMNS
BY HENRY WILSON

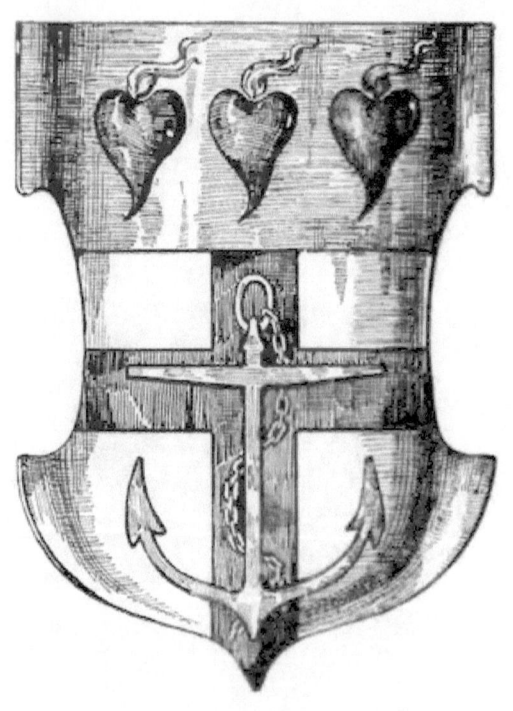

COSTUMES.

15. THE PROLOCUTOR. BY SELWYN IMAGE.
16. TRUEHEARTE THE KNIGHT. BY WALTER CRANE.
17. ASCHEMON THE DRAGON. BY WALTER CRANE.
18. FAYREMONDE. BY HENRY WILSON.
19. THE FAIR CITY OF ATHENS. BY WALTER CRANE.
20. THE FAIR CITY OF THEBES. BY HENRY HOLLIDAY.
21. THE FAIR CITY OF PARIS. BY E. R. HUGHES.
22. THE LAMP OF SACRIFICE. BY HENRY WILSON.
23. THE LAMP OF OBEDIENCE. BY HENRY WILSON.
24. DANTE. BY H. M. PAGET.
25. RAMESES II. BY HENRY HOLLIDAY.
26. KLEIO. BY HENRY HOLLIDAY.
27. TITIAN. BY HUGH STANNUS.
28. ALBERT DÜRER. BY WALTER CRANE.
29. DANTE ATTENDANT ON FLORENCE. BY C. R. ASHBEE.
30. TITIAN ATTENDANT ON VENICE. BY C. R. ASHBEE.
31. PHEIDÆUS ATTENDANT ON ATHENS. BY C. R. ASHBEE.
32. ST. LOUIS ATTENDANT ON PARIS. BY E. R. HUGHES.
33. PAGE ATTENDANT ON PARIS. BY E. R. HUGHES.
34. LONDON. BY WALTER CRANE.
35. DANCE OF THE FIVE SENSES. BY WALTER CRANE.
36. LABOUR. BY GERALD MOIRA.
37. INVENTION. BY GERALD MOIRA.
38. THE MONTHS. BY LOUIS DAVIS.
39. FREEDOM AND COMMERCE. BY WALTER CRANE.

The Prolocutor

TRUEHEARTE THE KNIGHT

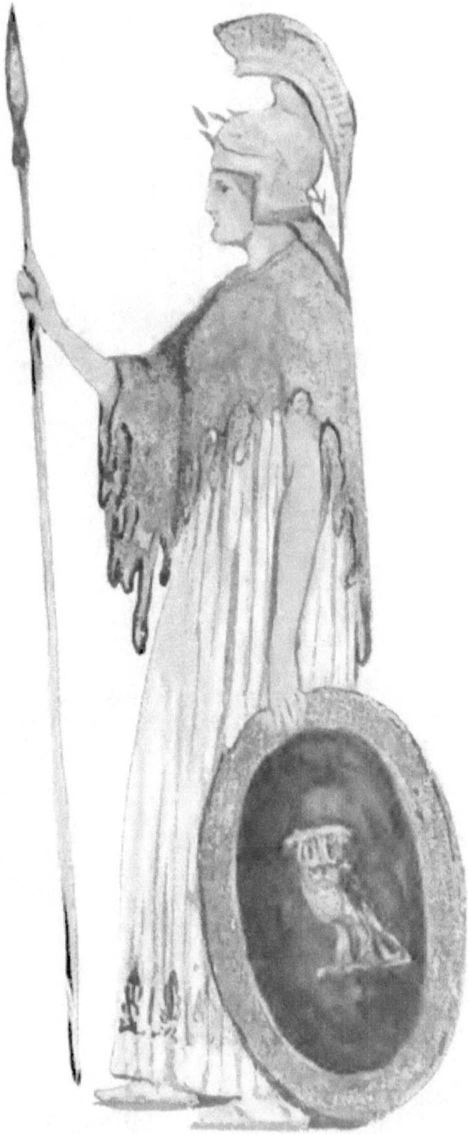

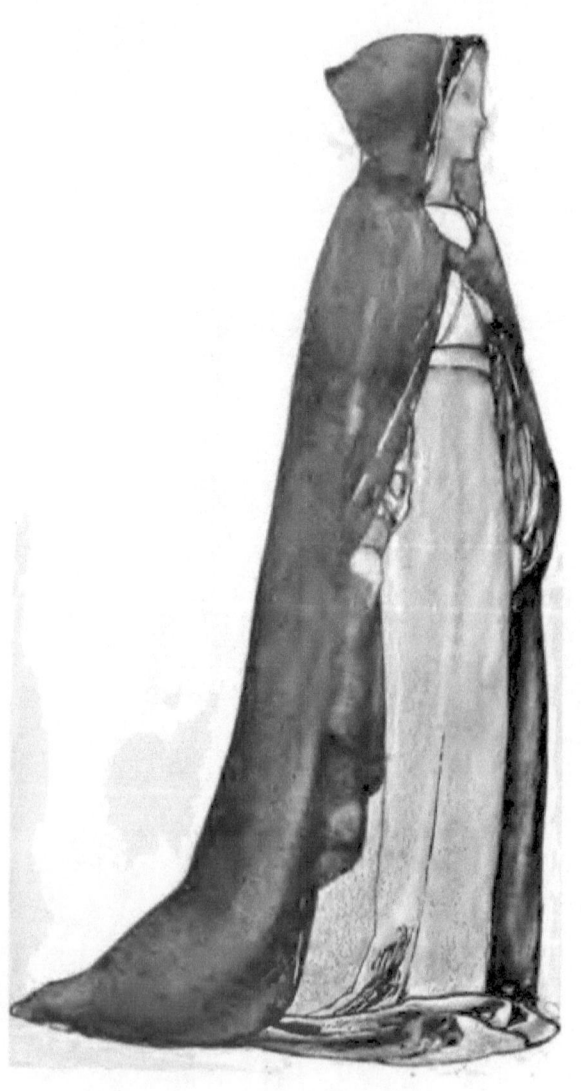

"THE LAMP OF OBEDIENCE"
BY HENRY WILSON

·ALBERT·DURER·

"VENICE AND TITIAN"
BY C. R. ASHBEE

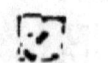

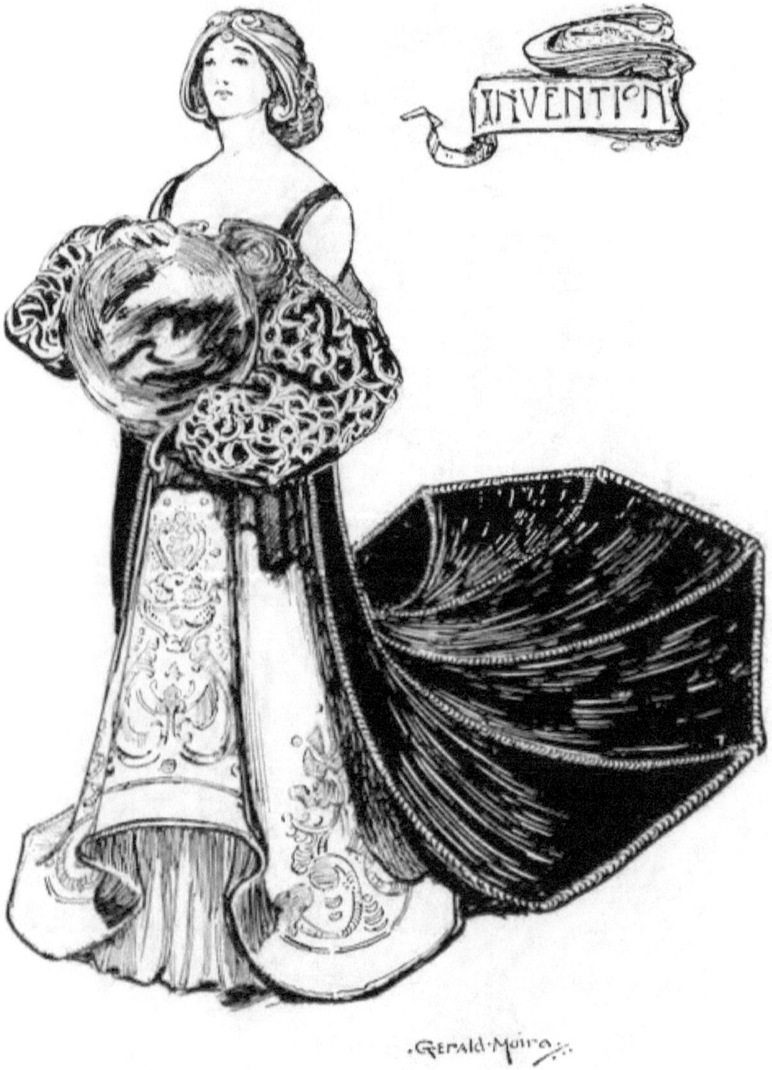
INVENTION
Gerald Moira

DEMONS.

40. THE LORD OF THE DEMONS. BY T. R. SPENCE.
41. SCAMPINUS. BY C. WHALL.
42. BUMBLEBEADALUS. BY C. WHALL.
43. CUPIDITAS. BY C. WHALL.
44. SLUMDRUM. BY C. WHALL.
45. SCAMPINUS. BY T. R. SPENCE.
46. DEMON. BY A. S. HAYNES.
47. DEMON. BY J. D. BATTEN.
48. BOGUS. BY C. R. ASHBEE.
49. THE RED DEMON. BY W. STRANG.

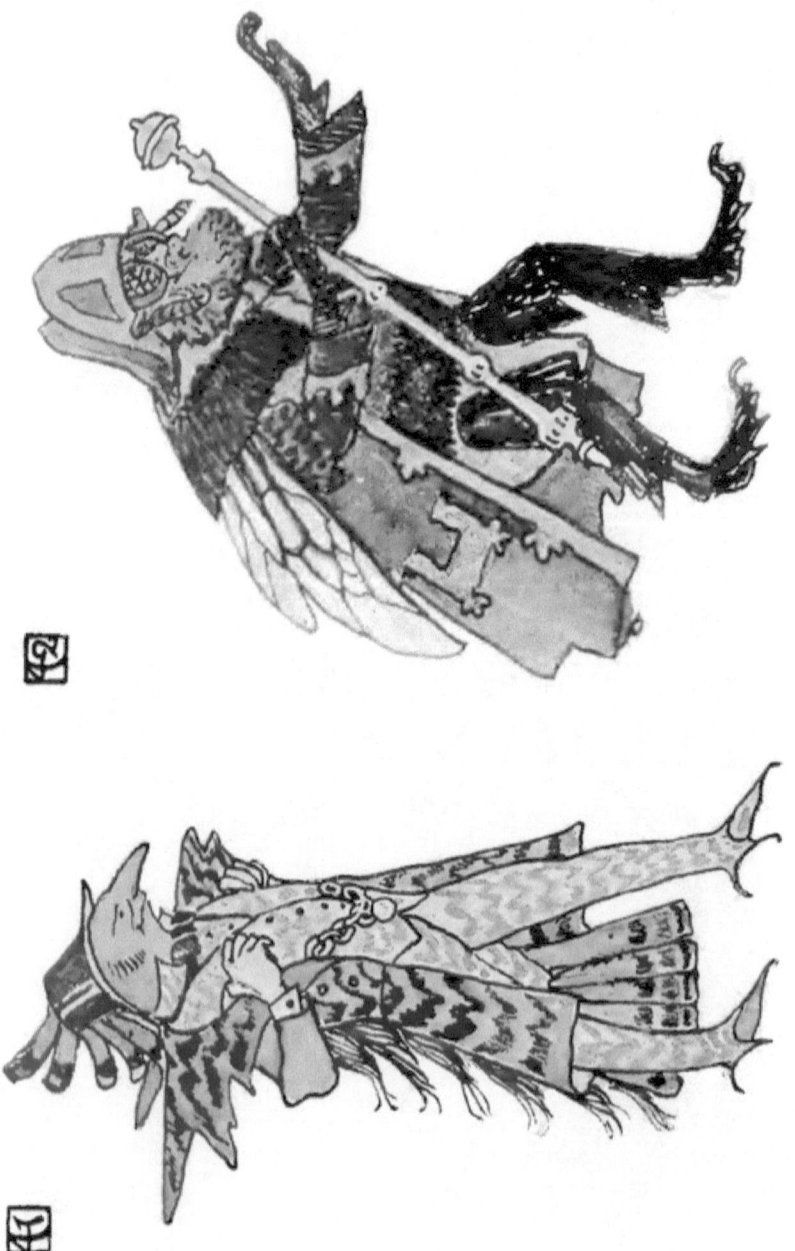

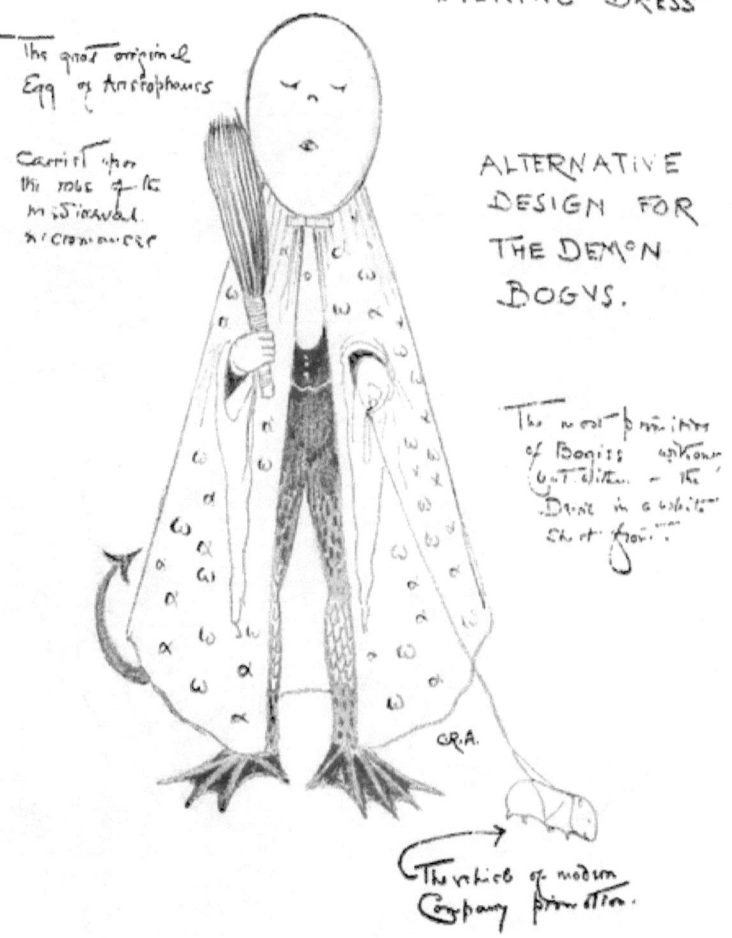

THE RED DEMON.

SUNDRY DRAWINGS.

50. GENIUS OF THE MASQUE. BY C. HOLROYD.
51. SPIRIT OF THE MASQUE. BY W. STRANG.
52. A DEMON IN MUFTI. BY L. RAVEN HILL.
53. CLIFFORD'S INN, THE HOME OF THE ART WORKERS' GUILD. BY T. R. WAY.
54. ENTRANCE TO CLIFFORD'S INN. BY JOSEPH PENNELL.
55. HALL, CLIFFORD'S INN. BY C. O. MURRAY.
56. REHEARSAL OF THE MASQUE AT STIRLING LEE'S STUDIO. BY F. W. LAWSON.
57. SKETCH FROM NELSON'S MONUMENT IN THE GUILD-HALL. BY BERESFORD PITE.
58 AND 59. OPENING BARS OF MUSIC. BY MALCOLM LAWSON. DRAWN BY PAUL WOODROFFE.

"Yes I'm a demon, don't you know!"

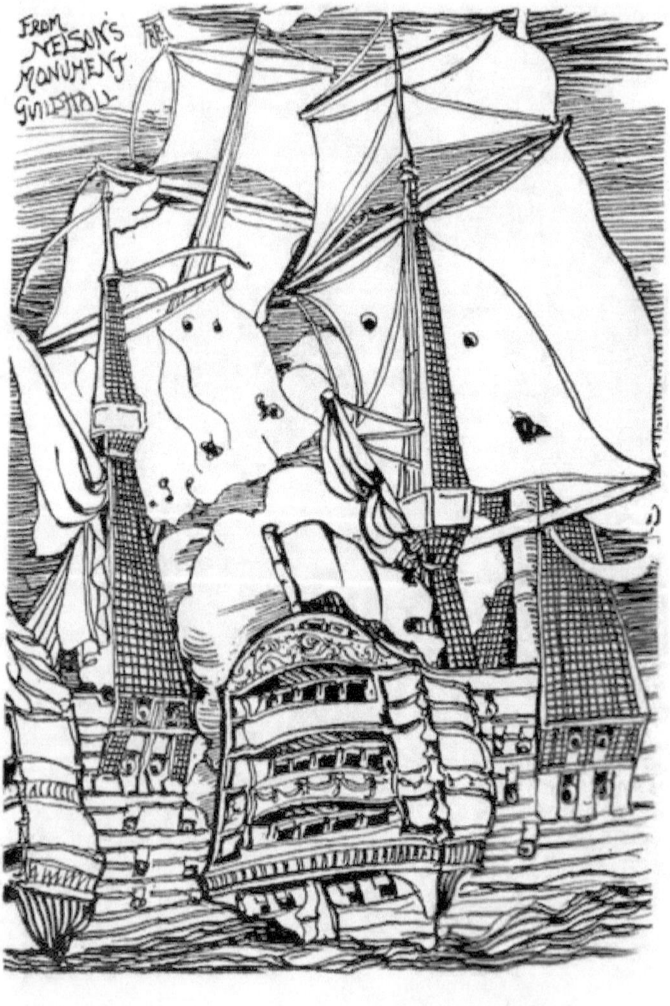
FROM NELSON'S MONUMENT. GUILDHALL

www.ingramcontent.com/pod-product-compliance
Lightning Source LLC
Chambersburg PA
CBHW021941160426
43195CB00011B/1184